AIR

All About Cyclones, Rainbows, Clouds, Ozone and More

David Allen

Illustrated by Gordon Bain

Greey de Pencier Books

Published 1993 by Greey de Pencier/Books from OWL.
Books from OWL are published in Canada by Greey de Pencier Books,
56 The Esplanade, Suite 302, Toronto, Ontario M5E 1A7
All rights reserved. No part of this book may be reproduced or copied in
any form without written permission from the publisher.

Published simultaneously in the United States by Firefly Books (U.S.) Inc.
P.O. Box 1338, Ellicott Station, Buffalo, NY 14205.
Originally published in Australia by Ellsyd Press.
Copyright © 1991 text and illustrations David Ell Press Pty Ltd

*OWL and the Owl colophon are trademarks of the Young Naturalist
Foundation. Greey de Pencier Books is a licensed user of trademarks
of the Young Naturalist Foundation.

Canadian Cataloguing in Publication Data

Allen, David A., 1946–
        Air: all about cyclones, rainbows, clouds, ozone and more

ISBN 1-895688-08-6

1. Air – Juvenile literature. 2. Cyclones –
Juvenile literature. 3. Rainbow – Juvenile
literature. 4. Clouds – Juvenile literature.
5. Ozone – Juvenile literature. I. Bain, Gordon.
II. Title.

QC161.2A55 1993   j533'.6   C92-095065-5

Cover design: Julia Naimska
Cover photo: Rick Rudnicki/First Light
Cover illustration: Gary Clement

Printed in Hong Kong
A   B   C   D   E   F   G

Contents

Can You Touch the Sky?

The blue sky looks like a ceiling, but it isn't. If you could fly straight up from the ground, you wouldn't find a solid ceiling to touch, just air all the way. Air isn't really blue. It just looks blue when the sun shines on it.

Air is all around you ... above, below, inside and out. It flows around you like water when you are swimming. It gets into every open space. You can only escape from air under water.

Water is made of tiny **molecules**. A molecule is the smallest bit that a drop of water can be broken up into. Molecules are so tiny that more than a million would fit across the width of one of the hairs on your head.

Air is made up of molecules too, but they are much further apart so we don't see or feel them in the way that we see and feel water. When molecules are so far apart we call them a **gas**.

There are several types of molecules in the air. If you could divide up a roomful of air you would find about 2280 parts **nitrogen** molecules, 630 parts **oxygen** molecules, and 30 parts **argon** molecules. Just one part would be **carbon dioxide**, a very important gas.

There are water molecules in air too, but they are so far apart that the water is a gas. We call it **water vapor**. In our roomful of air there are about 20 parts water molecules, but in hot, steamy regions of the world there can be as many as 50 parts water. In a cold, dry place like Antarctica there would be almost no water vapor, and our roomful of air would have more of the other types of molecules.

The air we breathe

All animals need oxygen to live. Humans are animals and so need it too. We breathe in air so that we can get the oxygen. In our lungs oxygen gets mixed into the blood and is carried to the muscles and brain where it is needed. At the same time, our body gets rid of carbon dioxide. The blood takes that to our lungs to breathe out. Every time we breathe we take some oxygen out of the air and put back some carbon dioxide.

If we breathe in a closed space such as a car with the windows shut, the amount of oxygen will slowly decrease and the amount of carbon dioxide will increase, so that our bodies will get less and less of the oxygen they need. We will become tired and sleepy, and we should open the windows. So why doesn't the whole atmosphere eventually run out of oxygen?

The answer is that plants keep the air fresh for us. They take in carbon dioxide and give out oxygen. If there were no plants, we would use up all the oxygen and die. For every one of us there must be many trees or hundreds of plants somewhere on earth to keep making oxygen.

= oxygen

= carbon dioxide

Weighing You Down

Like everything else, air has weight. Because the molecules are so much further apart than in water or a tree or a spoon, the weight seems very small. Even so, the air in your living room weighs about as much as your mom or dad.

If you put a postage stamp on your back lawn, the weight of the atmosphere above it, all the way from the ground to outer space, would be about 2 kg (almost 5 pounds). A large piece of paper may have nearly a tonne (2000 pounds) of air resting on it. You can feel this if you place a ruler on a table so that its end sticks out over the edge and then put a sheet of newspaper on top of it. Try to lift the paper by hitting the end of the ruler. You can't on account of the weight of the atmosphere on it.

Because air flows everywhere, the weight of the atmosphere is the same inside a house or out, and it presses onto everything whichever way up it is. The ceiling is pressed upwards by the atmosphere, but is pressed downwards just as much by the air above. If you lean gently on the ruler you give air a chance to pour in underneath the paper and push upwards as well as down. Then you can lift the paper easily.

Pressure

The way the air presses on everything is called **atmospheric pressure**. This is measured with a **barometer**. Do you have a barometer in your house?

The pressure of the air changes a little from day to day. Look at a barometer if you can. You'll probably find that it says the weather will be fine when the pressure is high and stormy when it is low. This isn't always right, but very often is.

If you go up a mountain, there is less atmosphere above you, so the pressure is lower. This also means that there is less air in the same space. If your house were on a high mountain, the air in your living room might weigh only half as much as your mom or dad.

Most mountaineers who climb high mountains like Everest have to carry extra oxygen in cylinders because if they go too high there isn't enough for them to breathe.

Hearing things

As well as giving us oxygen to live, air does another useful thing for us. When your mom calls you for dinner, it is air that carries the sound to you. Sound makes the molecules of air near her mouth jiggle back and forth so that they bump into others. These jostle the next set of molecules, and so on all the way to your ear.

If we lived in a world without air, we would never hear anything.

Feeling the Air

Although you can't see the air around you, you can feel it in several ways. For example, you can sense the temperature of the air.

Air molecules move around at 1500 km/h (930 mph), but they don't go very far because they are always bumping into one another or into something else. They move faster when they are warmer, and then bump into you harder. You feel that bumping as heat. When we say it is a hot day, it is really the warm air that we feel.

Hot and cold

The hottest places on earth are the deserts of North America, Africa, Arabia and Australia, where temperatures as high as 58°C (135°F) have been recorded. The coldest known place is Vostok station in Antarctica, where it can be nearly –90°C (–130°F).

Warm air isn't quite as heavy as cold air, so it rises slowly. Cold air comes down. When your home heating is on, you will find it warmest near the ceiling and coldest around your feet.

The wind

You can also feel the air on a windy day. If the wind is blowing faster than about 70 km/h (45 mph) it is called a gale force wind: if faster than about 90 km/h (55 mph) it is called storm force and can push you over. Winds have been measured up to more than 300 km/h (190 mph), strong enough to do a lot of damage.

An **anemometer** tells how fast the wind is blowing. The stronger the wind, the faster it spins.

Humid weather

There's another way you can feel the air. Sometimes it seems very dry, and at other times it is humid. When it is warm and humid we say the weather is sticky or muggy, and if it is cold and humid we say it is damp.

In these conditions, you are feeling the amount of water vapor in the air. Scientists measure this with a **hygrometer**, and weather forecasts report the humidity. We feel it to be dry if the humidity is less than 30 per cent, and damp or sticky if it is more than about 70 per cent. When air warms up its humidity lessens, and when it cools the humidity rises. If the humidity reaches 100 per cent then it will be misty or foggy. One hundred per cent humidity means that no more water vapor will fit into the air.

When the Wind Blows

Wind is air moving between places with different pressure. If you blow up a balloon, the air pressure is higher inside than out. Let go of the neck and air rushes out until the pressure is the same inside and out. On earth, air is constantly on the move from high pressure regions to areas of low pressure.

At the equator the sun's intense heat warms large amounts of air. This makes the air lighter, so it rises, spreading out to north and south, leaving behind a low-pressure area. As it moves outward, the warm air cools and sinks toward the ground, creating areas of high pressure near the tropics of Cancer and Capricorn. Some of this air moves back toward the equator, but some continues onward.

At the poles the opposite happens. There the air is very cold and heavy. It pushes down, creating an area of high pressure. This cold air spreads outward toward areas of low pressure, getting warmer and beginning to rise as it moves. Some of this air turns back toward the poles, but some continues outward.

In the mid-areas between the equator and the poles, air masses of different temperatures and pressures meet. Here the weather changes often, one day stormy and cold, the next sunny and calm.

As you can see below, all of these winds blow at an angle. Why? Because the earth is turning under them.

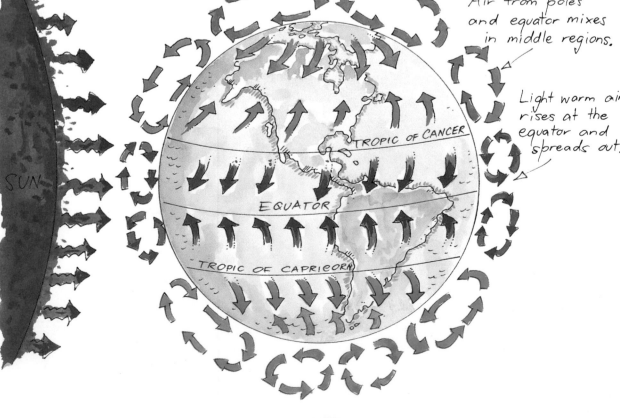

Heavy cold air flows down and outward from the polar regions.

Air from poles and equator mixes in middle regions.

Light warm air rises at the equator and spreads out.

SUN

TROPIC OF CANCER

EQUATOR

TROPIC OF CAPRICORN

Blowing round in circles

Large masses of high and low pressure air meet about halfway between the poles and the equator, where air is trying to move in from both north and south. The wind blows around and around in huge circles, like a dog chasing its tail. As these air masses move around the earth they make big changes in the weather every few days in parts of the world such as North America, Europe, and southern Australia.

Sometimes the wind goes around in circles very fast. These giant, spinning, low-pressure storms are called **hurricanes, typhoons** or **tropical cyclones**. They form over oceans, usually in late summer, and cause a lot of damage especially if they move into cities. Hurricane Andrew caused tremendous damage when it passed through the state of Florida and other parts of the United States.

Smaller twisting winds can make **water spouts** and lift water from the ocean to the clouds. Over land these become **tornadoes**, lifting soil, rocks, trees or houses into the air. Some scientists think that winds in tornadoes are as fast as 1000 km/h (over 600 mph).

In some countries, baby tornadoes are common on warm days in open spaces away from trees and buildings. Called **dust devils**, these tiny whirlwinds scurry by, carrying little swirls of earth or sand.

Riding on the Wind

Letting the wind work for us

A strong wind can be very useful. The invention of windmills cut out the hard work of lifting water out of deep wells, while sailing ships saved people from having to row everywhere.

A sailboat is pushed in the direction the wind is blowing. By moving the sail, the skipper can travel across the wind, and even partly towards it. It just needs some wind to fill the sail so that there is more air pressure behind the sail than in front of it.

The blades of a windmill are tilted sideways to catch the wind. This makes them go around. The turning blades work a pump to lift water up a pipe from deeper underground than we can dig wells. In windy places another type of windmill is used to make electricity; this is called a wind generator.

A fan or a propellor is just like a windmill going backwards and making wind.

A kite works just like the sail of a yacht. It is tilted so that air pushes it upwards into the sky.

A parachute lets someone fall slowly from an airplane even if there isn't any wind. As they fall, air gets trapped in the parachute. There is more air pressure below the parachute pushing it up than above it pushing down, so they float to the ground.

Flying

When the propellor of an airplane turns, it pulls the plane forwards, and air rushes past the wings. All wings have a special shape, flat on the bottom, rounded on top. Air that flows underneath travels almost in a straight line, but air going over the top has to flow up at the front and down again at the rear. Because the journey is longer, the air has to go faster over the top. Faster air makes a lower pressure above the wing and higher pressure underneath, which pushes the airplane up into the sky.

Frisbees are rounded on top to work the same way. They float through the air as long as they are moving forwards. If a frisbee tips over a little, the pressure pushes it in a curve instead of just holding it up. Try it.

Gliders and hang-gliders don't have motors, so they have to find places where warm air is rising from the ground. They can move from one rising patch to another without going down much because as they move forwards they are pushed upwards by the action of the air over their wings, just like an airplane or a frisbee.

Birds, bats and insects use many tricks to fly. To make it easier, they aren't very heavy. Dogs and eagles are about the same size, but a medium-sized dog weighs as much as three or four eagles.

Birds twist their feathers when they fly. When they lift their wings the air flows through, and when they lower their wings it doesn't. That way they push themselves upwards. Some birds glide on rising warm-air currents.

Castles in the Sky

Do you ever sit and watch clouds? Normally they don't seem to change while you watch, but if you look away for a minute and then look back they can look different. Clouds are always moving slowly, sometimes growing bigger and sometimes disappearing into blue sky. Do you see patterns in the clouds? A lion, a tree, or an old man? Or do they look like castles?

Clouds often appear solid when seen from above. From an airplane clouds look as though they'd be fun to roll around on and jump in. But clouds aren't solid, and although they float in the sky you would fall right through one.

What are clouds made of?

All clouds are made of the same thing — tiny droplets of water. A mirror in your bathroom becomes covered with water after you've had a shower because the little droplets settle on it.

Drops of water fall from a tap, but in a cloud the drops are really tiny and can hang in the air for a long time. Warm air rising from hot ground can carry the droplets upwards. That is why clouds often grow taller as you watch. Fog and mist are clouds on the ground. If air never rose, the ground would be covered by a permanent fog.

Even air that feels dry can make clouds if it rises high enough. As it moves upwards it gets colder, and water drops form in it just as when you breathe on a cold window. Clouds often form over mountains because the wind is pushed upwards to higher, colder levels.

How big is a cloud?

Clouds are bigger than you might think. Watch for their shadows on a hillside: the shadow is the same size as the cloud. Even quite a small cloud can be as heavy as ten large elephants, although it is made of droplets so small that you would need a magnifying glass to see one.

High-flying aircraft often leave long white **contrails**, which are just a type of cirrus cloud.

Cirrus clouds are the white, wispy ones that move very slowly indeed and have fuzzy edges.

Stratus clouds are big sheets of hazy gray clouds that cover most of the sky. You can often see a fuzzy sun through stratus clouds even though they may be 1 km (over half a mile) thick.

Cumulus clouds are small, fluffy and usually white. These are the clouds you see against a blue sky on sunny afternoons.

Cumulus and some stratus clouds are made of water. Other stratus and all cirrus clouds form farther above the ground where the temperature is well below freezing. There the droplets of water freeze to become tiny crystals of ice. You can usually tell whether a cloud is made of ice crystals or water droplets if you can see its edge. Water clouds have proper edges but ice clouds fade away into blue sky.

Umbrella Weather

On a sunny day, water spilled on the sidewalk dries up quickly. The water **evaporates** into the air. Washing dries on the line in the same way. The sun is always trying to dry up the oceans and seas, so water keeps evaporating from them. Warm air carries the water vapor up to make clouds.

The droplets in a cloud meet and join together to make bigger and bigger drops. The drops become so heavy that they fall down as rain.

When rain falls on land it starts to flow back to the oceans along streams and rivers. In the end, that same water will be evaporated again to make more rain. This is the **evaporation cycle**, and if it didn't occur there would be no rain and all land would be a sandy desert.

Ice crystals in very high clouds can also grow big enough to fall. They can land as soft flakes of snow or as hailstones, depending on what sort of cloud they fall out of. Often raindrops started out as snow or ice and melted on the way down.

The morning dew

It doesn't have to rain or snow for water to fall out of the sky. At night the air cools, and has to get rid of some of the water vapor that it gained by evaporation during the day. The water settles as very fine drops of dew. On cold nights the dew freezes to make a white frost and we say that Jack Frost has visited.

Thunderstorms

When the ground is very hot, clouds rise high into the air and thunderstorms can occur. It's dangerous to be near a tree or building that is struck by lightning, so stay inside during a storm. And don't use a telephone. You can watch a thunderstorm safely through a closed window in a building.

Can you see that the lightning flashes several times very quickly along the same path? Lightning is electricity that's made when air rises and falls. Every second there are about 100 flashes of lightning somewhere on the earth. The electricity moves so fast that it would take a flash only one second to cross the country if it could jump that far.

Thunder is the sound made by lightning. Unless the flash is very close, you hear the thunder later because sound moves more slowly than light. Thunder rumbles for a long time because you first hear the bang from the bottom of the flash, and then from higher up.

You can tell how far away a flash of lightning was. Count the seconds between seeing the flash and hearing the thunder start. To figure the distance in kilometres, divide the number by three. (For miles, divide by five.)

Some thunderclouds have flat tops

EEEEEK !!!

So do some humans!

17

Will it be Sunny Today?

Many people grumble that weather forecasts are always wrong. In fact we should be pleased at how well the weather can be forecast, because it is difficult to do. It is very hard to tell how much evaporation there will be, and how much air will rise during the day to make clouds and rain. This is most true near oceans and seas, where the air is damper.

Clouds act like a blanket over the earth keeping us warm at night, and like a sunshade by day keeping us cool. So if we don't know how much cloud there will be, we can't predict the temperatures very well either.

We can predict the weather more easily in some places. People who live near the equator know that it rains almost every afternoon. This is because damp air rises there as the ground heats up. Dense jungles grow near the equator. The same air has no water left by the time it comes down at the tropics, which is why there are deserts in north and south Africa, in Australia and in the Americas. It doesn't often rain in those deserts. In some parts of the Atacama Desert in Chile it has never been known to rain.

We also know it will be cold over the poles because the sun never gets high in the sky to warm the ground. Weather forecasting is hard between the tropics and the polar regions.

Weather maps

Patterns of weather move around the world, so it's easier to predict what will happen if there are reports from many places, including ships at sea. From these reports a **meteorologist** makes a map showing what the air pressure, wind, cloud and rain are doing over part of the earth.

Weather satellites take photographs from about 36,000 km (22,300 miles) above the earth, and the pictures show where the clouds are.

Usually weather features move from west to east (from left to right on the map), but they change as they go, especially when they cross from land to ocean or ocean to land, or when they run into each other.

Warm fronts are shown with rounded bumps, cold fronts with pointed ones.

Cool dry air from Arctic.

These lines show where rain or snow is falling

Cool moist air from the Pacific.

Warm dry air from desert regions.

Warm wet air from the Gulf of Mexico.

Winds move out from areas of high pressure (H) and in towards areas of low pressure (L).

Dirty Air

We hear a lot about pollution, but do you know what it means? When you peel an orange you spray molecules of oil into the air that push away some of the normal air molecules. Anyone nearby will smell the orange. Do you think you have polluted the air in this case?

Anything that you or other people add to the air is pollution. Most people don't mind the smell of oranges, but some of the things we put into the air will harm either us or other living things, so we must avoid that sort of pollution.

Smoke and dust

Smoke is a type of pollution. It comes from fires, cigarettes, factories and cars whose engines need repairing. The molecules in smoke have joined together into lumps big enough to see through a microscope, and sometimes even without one. Dust is made of lumps too.

Smoke and dust get stuck in the tiny tubes of your lungs, especially if you breathe through your mouth. Whenever a tube is blocked, that's one place less for oxygen to get into your body. If you breathe smoke for many years your lungs could be so blocked that you get breathless when you do any exercise.

Some diseases are caused by dirt in your lungs. The dust from asbestos and the smoke from cigarettes (even from someone else's cigarettes) are very bad for you. Many people die every year from lung cancer, probably caused by cigarette smoke.

Gases that harm

Some gases just smell bad; others are poisonous. Carbon monoxide is poisonous, though you can't smell it. It's made in fires and by cars and trucks. Lead is another poison made by cars that use leaded gasoline. It's unhealthy for you to breathe exhaust fumes.

When the sun shines on car exhaust gases it turns them into **smog**, which is also bad for you. Do you ever smell smog where you live?

The gases from cars and factories get into clouds and make **acid rain**. This can kill the trees and plants it falls on. Acid rain can even dissolve buildings over a long time.

The greenhouse effect

Almost everything we burn makes carbon dioxide. More and more carbon dioxide is getting into the atmosphere. Scientists worry that this is making the world warmer because carbon dioxide stops heat from escaping, just like the glass windows in a greenhouse.

If the world gets warmer, the weather will change everywhere. This might mean we can't grow the food we need, it might make the sea rise and swamp many cities, and it could spread more diseases.

The ozone hole

Ozone is a special type of oxygen molecule high up in the air. It stops the sun's ultraviolet light from burning us. Scientists are worried that the ozone is disappearing because we are polluting the air with gases called CFCs. CFCs have been used in spray cans and refrigerators, but many countries have agreed to stop using them, because if ozone is destroyed more people might get skin cancer, and some plant life may be destroyed.

High Above Our Heads

If you could become an astronaut and zoom away from the earth, what would the atmosphere be like as you went through it? Long ago people could tell only by going up mountains. They found that as they went higher, there was less air to breathe, it was colder, and usually it was more windy. So they thought the atmosphere got colder all the way into outer space.

When rockets and weather balloons were used to carry thermometers high into the air, scientists found that the atmosphere isn't that way at all. There are several layers in the atmosphere, one on top of the other.

This is the stratosphere. You would find it getting slowly warmer if you went up through the stratosphere, until at its top the temperature would be about the same as on the ground. The stratosphere contains the important gas ozone that stops the sun's ultraviolet light from burning us.

Oh no!! The jet stream!

This is called the troposphere. The highest mountains are in the troposphere, and it gets colder as you go up through it, as cold as −50°C (−60°F).

It gets colder as you go up through the next layer called the exosphere. This is where most satellites orbit the earth. There are almost no molecules of air left this far up. As you go higher, the exosphere gets thinner and thinner until finally it turns into outer space.

It gets hot as you go up through the ionosphere. In fact it is hotter than molten iron here. You wouldn't feel the heat though because there is so little air that you wouldn't be thumped by lots of molecules the way you are on the ground.

Because the ionosphere is so hot, the gas molecules are altered. They look the same to us, but they behave as mirrors to radio waves. We can get radio signals from a long way away because the waves bounce off the ionosphere, just as you can see round a bend using a mirror.

Airplanes fly in the stratosphere. They sometimes find a very strong wind called the jet stream. This wind always blows from the west towards the east, and is only found about halfway between the equator and the poles, over places such as North America, Europe and southern Australia. The jet stream is never in quite the same place from one day to the next. Pilots like to find the jet stream if they are flying east, but want to avoid it when they fly west.

Colors in the Sky

Do you know that there are several rainbows that you can see at the same time?

To see a rainbow you must stand with your back to the sun and the sun should be shining on drops of water. Usually the drops are falling rain. The colors are made by sunlight going into the raindrops and coming out again. Light going into a glass prism also makes rainbow colors.

The drops don't have to be rain. A garden sprinkler or a waterfall make rainbows too. You can sometimes see drops of dew on a branch or a spider's web turn rainbow colors when the sun shines through them.

The colors of the rainbow are said to be red, orange, yellow, green, blue, indigo and violet.

Most people don't see indigo and violet at all, or if they do, both look the same color. All these colors make up the **spectrum**.

A legend says that if you dig at the foot of a rainbow you'll find a pot of gold. Of course there isn't really any gold, and this is just a way of saying that you can never get to the foot of a rainbow. If you walk towards a rainbow it just moves away, because there always has to be enough rain in front of you for the rainbow to form.

This is the secondary bow.

This is the primary bow.

These are called supernumerary bows. They are closer together if the raindrops are big.

The sky between the bows is darker than sky outside them.

Rings round things

There are other things like rainbows to watch for. You may see faint colored rings around the sun or moon when they shine through fog or cloud. This is called a **corona**. Just like the extra bows below a rainbow, the bands are closer together if the droplets are big. If large and small droplets are all mixed together, the corona will be white.

Coronas and rainbows are made by water droplets, but clouds with ice crystals in them also make colored patterns. One pattern that is made by ice is a big circle round the moon. Have you ever seen it?

Another colored pattern made by ice crystals is a **sun dog**. You will see the sun dog when the sun is low in the sky and a cloud of ice crystals is to one side. If the rainbow colors are very bright in the sun dog, then the crystals of ice must all be a bit bigger than the period at the end of this sentence. If you looked at the crystals under a microscope, they would be flat and have six sides, like this:

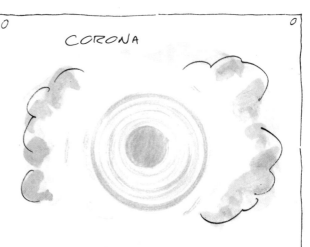

CORONA

CORONA

A sun dog is as far from the sun as the big circle is from the moon - a bit more than the span of your hand at arm's length.

Twinkle, Twinkle

Have you noticed how a straight straw looks bent in your glass of water or lemonade? The straw isn't really bent but it looks as though it is because of the way light moves.

Light usually travels straight to our eyes from whatever we see. But when light comes out of water it makes a sharp bend, so we think it has come from a different direction. This bending is called **refraction**.

Where you *think* the star is.

Where the star really is.

The atmosphere acts like the water, though the refraction bend is smaller. When a star is near the horizon, its light is bent by the atmosphere so that we see it higher in the sky than it really is. As the star sets lower in the west, the refraction becomes bigger because we are looking through more air.

When the sun or moon is almost at the horizon, refraction affects its bottom edge much more strongly than its top. This is why it looks as though its bottom edge is being pushed upwards at the moment of sunset or moonset.

A toaster experiment

Hot air makes less refraction than cold air, so if there are areas of hot and cold in the atmosphere, light may get bent in different ways. As these areas of warm and cool air move, things seen through the air seem to shimmer to and fro. You can see this by looking over the top of a toaster as it is cooking. If the sun is shining past the toaster, you can see the shadow of the hot air rising from it.

After a sunny day, warm air rises from the ground, and things you see through that air will shimmer. This is why stars seem to twinkle. The more areas of warm and cool air that are swirling about, the more the stars twinkle. They twinkle most when they are near the horizon, where there is more air to look through.

Refraction also makes the lights of a city twinkle on a warm evening.

Is It Dark at Night?

Do you think it gets dark at night? Really dark? It doesn't. However dark it seems, if you stay out of doors long enough your eyes become used to the dark. Then you can see that things like trees look blacker than the sky. That means the sky can't be completely dark.

Many things stop the sky getting dark at night. The moon and city lights are the main reasons. If you live near a city, the light from street lamps and buildings reflect off the smoke, haze and dust in the air to make the sky bright. Even if you get away from the city lights there is still the light of the stars.

There are also lots of tiny flashes of light in the sky. We can't see the flashes, though scientists can detect them with their instruments. They combine to make the sky glow. They are made of harmful rays travelling through space. The rays are even harsher than X-rays, but our atmosphere stops them from hitting us. It gives off a flash every time it stops one of these rays. Scientists use special telescopes to study these flashes.

The glow-in-the-dark sky

Strangest of all the things that stop the sky from getting dark is that the air actually glows. Electricity makes the gas in a fluorescent light glow, and there is a type of electricity that comes from the sun and flows into the top of the earth's atmosphere to make it glow, with a pale green light. Even when the sun goes down, the air still glows, just like glow-in-the-dark paint. This is called **fluorescence**.

Sometimes there is a big electrical storm on the sun, making the air glow very brightly indeed. Patches and streaks of red or green appear and disappear very quickly in the sky. Oxygen and nitrogen make these colors. This is an **aurora**, and it can cover the whole sky with bright colors in beautiful patterns that change as you watch.

Aurorae are best seen from the Arctic or from Antarctica, and they are most common when the sun has many sunspots on it. The airglow and the aurora both occur about 100 km (60 miles) above our heads, in the ionosphere.

Care for the Air

You can't smell clean, fresh air. Yet when you breathe it you feel good. If you breathe smoke, smog or harmful gases you feel bad. You have less energy. Your eyes might sting and your chest might ache. This is your body's way of telling you it doesn't like the air you are breathing.

Having fresh air to breathe isn't the only reason to look after the earth's atmosphere. If the ozone layer gets too thin, or if acid rain keeps on falling, or if too much carbon dioxide is made, humans might find life much more difficult and unpleasant.

We make carbon dioxide in our cars and factories. But we are killing the trees that turn it back into oxygen for us. Every year thousands and thousands of trees are cut down to make paper. Do you get lots of advertising and junk mail at your house? Trees are being killed to produce it.

When forests are cut down, there aren't as many trees to clean the air. Trees also make it cooler in summer, and help stop the wind from causing a lot of damage.

For all these reasons it is important to start taking better care of our air.

Do the right thing for the air

Here are some ways you can help keep the atmosphere in good condition for when you grow old, and for when your children and grandchildren grow old. Try to do as many of these things as you can, and try to persuade your parents and friends to do the same.

Some of these things might cost a little more money, but others will save you money. Which ones save money?

- Don't burn things unless you really have to.
- Try to use less electricity in your home whenever possible.
- Don't heat your house so much. Wear a sweater instead.
- Don't throw away pieces of paper until you've used them all you can.
- Recycle paper and cardboard. Use recycled paper. Check that your school recycles its paper.
- Don't go by car if you can walk or ride a bicycle. Share car rides when you can.
- Don't harm trees. Plant another tree.
- If you see factories making smoke, write to ask if it's pollution-free. If they don't write back, complain to your local council or federal government.

Other Worlds

This book is about the air on our own planet. What would we find on other worlds?

Smaller worlds like the moon don't have any air at all. If you took some air to the moon and let it go, it would float away just like helium-filled balloons on earth float off into the sky if you let them go.

Other planets that are big enough to have their own atmospheres don't have much oxygen in them. This is because plants don't grow there. The earth's atmosphere used to have no oxygen, but plants changed all that.

On Mars there is a very thin atmosphere of carbon dioxide and only a tiny bit of water. Clouds occasionally form on Mars, but they don't last long.

Venus is a planet as big as the earth. Its atmosphere is very thick and almost pure carbon dioxide. There's so much atmosphere that you would be squashed by it if you went there. At the same time the greenhouse effect makes the surface hotter than an oven, so you'd be roasted too. And the clouds are made of sulphuric acid, so if it ever rains there it will be very acid rain that falls.

There's no doubt that it's best here on earth where the air is still sweet!

Look! That pretty blue planet is turning brown!